FARM ANIMALS

CATTLE

Ann Larkin Hansen
ABDO Publishing Company

visit us at
www.abdopub.com

Published by Abdo Publishing Company 4940 Viking Drive, Edina, Minnesota 55435.
Copyright © 1998 by Abdo Consulting Group, Inc. International copyrights reserved in all countries. No part of this book may be reproduced in any form without written permission from the publisher.

Printed in the United States.

Cover Photo credits: Peter Arnold, Inc.
Interior Photo credits: Peter Arnold, Inc.

Edited by Lori Kinstad Pupeza

Library of Congress Cataloging-in-Publication Data

Hansen, Ann Larkin.
    Cattle / Ann Larkin Hansen
    p. cm. -- (Farm animals)
    Includes index.
    Summary: Describes the physical characteristics, habits, uses, and needs of the biggest, most important, and most common farm animal in the United States.
    ISBN 1-56239-603-X
    1. Cattle--Juvenile literature. 2. Dairy cattle--Juvenile literature. [1. Cattle. 2. Dairy cattle.] I. Title. II. Series: Hansen, Ann Larkin. Farm animals.
    SF197.5.H36   1998
    636.2--dc20
                                          95-52346
                                          CIP
                                          AC

About the Author

Ann Larkin Hansen has a degree in history from the University of St. Thomas in St. Paul, Minnesota. She currently lives with her husband and three boys on a farm in northern Wisconsin, where they raise beef cattle, chickens, and assorted other animals.

Contents

Cattle

One of the most peaceful sounds in the world is **cows** munching hay. The barn is quiet and cozy as night settles over the farm. For thousands of years, farmers have heard these sounds as they milked and fed their herds.

Cattle give us milk, beef, and leather. In many parts of the world they are still used to pull farm equipment. They are the most important and common farm animal in the United States. They are also the biggest.

Opposite page: Cows grazing in a meadow.

How Cattle
Were Tamed

Ten thousand years ago, herds of six-foot (two-meter) high **Aurochs** cattle roamed the plains of Central Asia. Following them were tribes of human hunters. Slowly, the hunters learned to herd, and make the cattle follow them. Soon the hunters became farmers, and they herded cattle to all parts of the world.

At first, these cattle were used only for meat. But about five thousand years ago, farmers began to milk the **cows**. They also invented the **yoke** at about the same time, so that cattle could pull wagons and plows.

A cattle ranch in Montana.

Breeds

About two hundred years ago, farmers began to **breed** cattle to do just one thing. Some cattle were bred to make lots of milk. Others were bred to make lots of meat. Today there are more than 100 different breeds.

Most breeds are either dairy or beef. **Dairy cattle** are tall and bony, with large **udders** where the milk is stored. **Beef cattle** are shorter, and more square and heavy.

Opposite page: A cow from France bred just for milking.

What They're Like

Cattle are big. Even the smallest weigh about 800 pounds (363 kilograms), and some **breeds** can be well over 1,500 pounds (680 kilograms). Some have horns, and some are **polled**, or without horns. They have split hooves and long tails with a bush of hair on the end. They moo when they're hungry or thirsty or upset.

Cattle have no upper front teeth, and cannot bite things. With their long, rough tongues, they grab and tear grass. As they graze, their long tails and big ears swish flies away.

Opposite page: A longhorn bull from England.

How Cattle Eat

After cattle have grazed for a few hours, they all lay down together. One by one they burp up balls of grass from their **rumens**, or first stomachs. They chew these balls well, then swallow them down to be fully digested in the next three stomachs. This is called chewing **cud**. All animals that have four stomachs and chew their cud are called **ruminants**.

A **cow's** rumen can hold forty gallons (151 liters) or more of food!

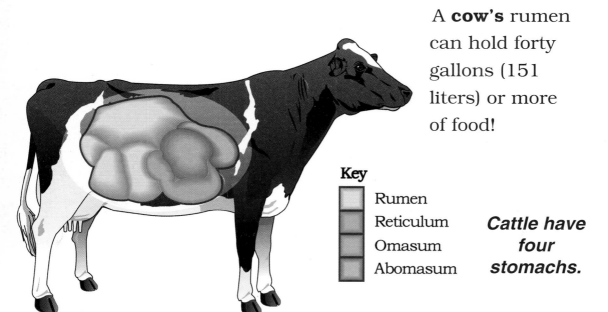

Key

- Rumen
- Reticulum
- Omasum
- Abomasum

Cattle have four stomachs.

Cows grazing in the early morning.

Dairy Cattle

Only **cows**, the females, can give milk. Dairy cows are milked twice each day with special machines. Because their bodies are working so hard to make a lot of milk, they must eat a lot. Dairy cows are fed grain, hay, and **silage** in the barn. In warm weather, they are turned out to pasture.

Dairy cows give a lot of milk! One Holstein cow can give more than 55,000 pounds (25,000 kilograms) in one year. That equals more than 6,800 gallons (25,738 liters)! Imagine how much ice cream, butter, yogurt, and cheese that could make!

The chain leashes hold the cows in place while they are milked.

Beef Cattle

Beef cattle are usually tougher than dairy **cows**. They are mostly kept outside, sometimes in a shed for very bad weather. They eat more grass and hay and less grain than dairy cows.

In the western states, large herds of beef cattle graze on ranges. They make use of land that is too dry, rocky, or hilly for other crops. Many ranchers still use horses and cowboys for rounding up their cattle in rough country.

Opposite page: Beef cattle being herded.

Caring for Cattle

Cattle are easy to care for, but they take a lot of space. In the eastern United States, as little as two acres will feed a **cow** and her **calf**. But in many western states, 40 acres are needed since there is so little rain to make the grass grow.

If cattle have enough grass, the only other things they really need are clean water, salt, and minerals. If the farmer wants a cow to give more milk, or grow faster, then grain and **silage** are fed also.

Cattle also need good fences. If the fences are weak, cattle will knock them down and wander away.

Cattle need a lot of space and water.

Handling Cattle

Because cattle are so big and strong, they can be very dangerous. Even though most **cows** are very gentle, they can knock you down just by swinging their heads. They don't bite, but they do kick. **Bulls** will attack people unexpectedly.

Dairy cows are trained to stand quietly in their stalls, and to be led by ropes. **Beef cattle** are herded through **chutes** and **corrals** when they need to be given shots or sorted into groups. Farmers must always be careful when handling cattle.

Opposite page: Cattle are big and strong and spend most of their time grazing in fields.

Cattle Health

Cattle are given shots to prevent sickness. They also must be **wormed** regularly to kill parasites. Parasites are little animals that live on other animals. Cattle can get sick from parasites.

Sometimes their hooves must be trimmed, just like people cut their fingernails.

Dairy **cows** must be kept very clean so their milk does not get **contaminated**. Their **udders** are washed before each milking. The milking machines are cleaned carefully after each use.

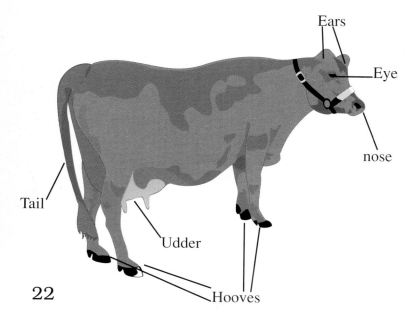

Ears

Eye

nose

Tail

Udder

Hooves

A dairy cow and her calf.

Calves

Cows take nine months to have a **calf**. The calf is born either on clean pasture grass, or on thick straw in a pen in the barn.

The wet, wiggly calf takes a few minutes to figure out how to work its legs. Then it begins to **nurse**, while the cow licks it dry. The calf is shy, but curious, just like its mother.

Opposite page: Calves learn to walk the same day they are born. This calf is competing at a county fair.

How Calves Grow Up

Calves are clumsy and soft, and they soon learn to come for a bucket of milk. They like to run and jump and butt their heads together. At about two weeks, they start to nibble on grass and grain. Dairy calves are **weaned** at about two months. Beef calves **nurse** for four months or longer.

Calves like to suck your fingers. Their tongues feel like slimy sandpaper. They run away if you walk towards them, but if you hold still they will come and sniff you.

A calf is full-grown by the time it is about three years old.

Opposite page: Calves learn early how to drink milk from a bucket.

Glossary

Aurochs—A primitive species of cattle. Most cattle today are thought to be descended from this animal or its close relatives.

Beef Cattle—Cattle raised primarily for beef production.

Breed—Different types of the same animal, like different flavors of ice cream. To breed also means to raise in order to develop new or improved kinds.

Bulls—Male cattle.

Calf—Baby cattle.

Chute—A narrow, unroofed tunnel used for holding cattle for treatment or to sort them into different groups.

Contaminated (cun-TAM-ee-nay-ted)—When germs or dirt get into milk or other things.

Corral—Small fenced area for confining cattle, often attached to a chute.

Cows—Female cattle.

Cud—Food that cattle burp up from their first stomach in order to chew more thoroughly. This is necessary for proper digestion.

Dairy Cattle—Cattle raised primarily for milk production.

Nurse—When calves take milk from their mothers.

Polled—Without horns.

Rumen—The first of cattle's four stomachs. Used for storing food until it can be re-chewed and passed through the rest of the digestive system.

Ruminant—Any animal with four stomachs that chews cud.

Selective Breeding—Improving a plant or animal by using only the best ones for breeding.

Silage—Chopped grasses, clovers, or grains blown into a silo while still moist and packed tightly. An important feed for dairy cattle.

Udder—Where a cow's milk comes from. It is a large, bag-like organ that hangs between her two rear legs.

Wean—To take a calf away from its mother so it no longer gets milk.

Worm—To give medicine to kill parasites.

Yoke—A wooden implement worn over the necks or horns of oxen. The yoke is then hitched to a wagon or plow for the oxen to pull.

Internet Sites

The Virtual Farm
http://www.manawatu.gen.nz/~tiros/ftour1.htm
A very impressive display including photos and sound. This
site is all about dairy farming in New Zealand.

Museums in the Classroom
**http://www.museum.state.il.us/mic_home/newton/
project/**
Prairie chickens and the prairie in Illinois by Mrs.
Vanderhoof's third grade class and Mrs. Volk's fourth grade
science classes.

Goats
http://www.ics.uci.edu/~pazzani/4H/Goats.html
This site has photos, graphics, and sound. It has tons of
information on raising goats and it even has a goat game.

Virtual Pig Dissection
http://mail.fkchs.sad27.k12.me.us/fkchs/vpig/
Learn how to dissect a pig without hurting a pig. This is a
really cool site that gets a lot of traffic.

Sheep
http://www.ics.uci.edu/~pazzani/4H/Sheep.html
This site has everything you would want to know about
sheep. Why raising sheep is fun, the sounds sheep make,
sheep statistics, basic care, sheep supplies, and much more.

Castalia Llamas
http://www.rockisland.com/~castalia/cllama.html
Chosen as a hotsite, featured on TV, listed in Popular
Science's WebWatch. Full of llama facts, images and stories
to amuse and bewilder. This is a cool site, check it out.

*These sites are subject to change. Go to your favorite search
engine and type in "farm animals" for more sites.*

PASS IT ON
Tell Others What You Like About Animals!
To educate readers around the country, pass on interesting tips
about animals, maybe a fun story about your animal or pet, and
little-known facts about animals. We want to hear from you!
**To get posted on ABDO Publishings website,
E-mail us at "animals@abdopub.com"**

Index